Uncommon Blessings in a Common World

Uncommon Blessings in a Common World

By

Dr. Freddy B. Wilson

Published by Wilsonet Enterprises

135 Bonnie Lane | Fayetteville, Georgia 30215 USA

404-754-0858 |

Wilsonet Enterprises is committed to excellence. This book is dedicated to the men of the late family dog, Alex.

Cover design by Dr. Freddy B. Wilson

Cover photo by Terrance D. Wilson

Bio photo by Tim Rogers

Published in the United States of America

ISBN: 978-0-9987873-5-0

1. Religion / Christian Life / Personal Growth

2. Family And Relationship/General

18.5.22

Uncommon Blessings in a Common World

A search of GOOGLE defined the word common when used as an adjective as, "occurring, found, or done often; prevalent". The example they gave was, "salt and pepper are the two most common seasonings". A search of GOOGLE defined the word uncommon when used as an adjective as "out of the ordinary; unusual". The example they gave was, "prostate cancer is not uncommon in men over 60". When used as an adverb, they defined uncommon as "remarkably". The example they gave was, "he was uncommon afraid".

There are things in my life that I can truly call uncommon. I will further define them as uncommon blessings. I owe all my blessings to God. There's no doubt about it that without God, I would not have been able to accomplish or experience many things in my life. If you look closely, I am sure you can find something in your life that happened but you can't explain why. If you have a personal relationship with God, you can find many more examples of uncommon blessings in this common world. Psalms 103:3 tells us God has provided good things in life.

One of the first phenomenal thing I can recall where God blessed me tremendously was being accepted in the US Air Force Academy (USAFA) in 1977. If you knew the requirement to get into any of the service academies you'd know what an accomplishment that was, especially in 1977! At that time there was a very small number of minorities in the Air Force Academy. When I first approached my high school JROTC commander he thought it was a good idea and felt I was fully qualified. The only problem was I needed a congressional nomination and that was a tough thing to get so I submitted my package. I was told by many of my classmates that I shouldn't bother since it was a rare thing indeed for anyone to get into a service academy, much less a Black man. I felt God was leading me to do this so I proceeded with my dreams. I prayed that God be with me on my journey and He came through! God blessed me with a very competitive nomination. I found that no one from my high school, Black or White, had ever been accepted at the USAFA.

I left Atlanta in the summer of 1977 to attend the USAFA Prep School for a year before entering the full academy. I did well in the USAFA and became one of the cadet leaders. I made some poor decisions and was home sick so I made a decision to leave the academy just as I made upper classman. God was still with me when I found a job at the

Atlanta Airport. I realized that was not the job I wanted for my future and enlisted in the Air Force six months later.

I did well as an aircraft mechanic but later got accepted into my current career field as a federal investigator. I met my wife during my transition time into my new career field in 1988. "Your life in Christ can be the greatest story ever told" - Avalon – The Greatest Story song. When my wife and I got married, she already had one child (who is now our oldest). My wife had our eldest daughter by Caesarian Section. When we had been married for three years, my wife got pregnant with our second child, a son. We were told that once a woman had a child by C-section, her next deliveries had to be by C-section also. My wife was really concerned about having to have surgery. As we were praying about any future surgery, The Lord told me my wife would not have to have surgery but could have the baby naturally. I was happy to hear this but now I knew I had to assure my wife that she could have the baby naturally and then we would have to deal with the doctors.

My wife felt comfortable with the news but wondered how we would tell the doctor. Keep in mind this is my personal testimony and I am not telling anyone else to go against what a doctor tells them. We told the doctors our decision and why. The doctor told us about what we were expecting about having previously having a C-section but we were not distracted from what God had told me. The doctors finally agreed to go along with our wishes but kept a constant watch on my wife to make sure there were no complications. On delivery day, my wife had to have an episiotomy during birth but she delivered our son naturally. My wife has had two other deliveries (the last a set of twins) and she had them naturally. God is so good especially when you obey His will.

You Can Count on God's Promises

When I was young, my mother kept us in church. I knew she normally took us all but my most of my memories were from when it was just my youngest brother and I going to church with her and taking trips with the church. My mother's bringing me to church was an introduction to Christ but I knew just being there wasn't enough. I decided to give my life to Christ when I was 15 years old. This was not a result of any kind of pressure from my mother or the church. I just felt a yearning for wanting to get closer to God. Like any other teenager I got to live a normal life but I walked with reverence to God. Don't get me wrong, I made mistakes along the way but always turned to God for answers.

One thing I wanted to share here was one day the Lord spoke words to me that I didn't understand. I clearly understood what He said but I didn't understand why He was telling me this information. After all, I was only 15 years old! Clearly, God told me that one day I would have twin daughters. I asked God, what? I didn't understand for I was only 15 years old and hadn't thought of having kids yet. For that matter, marriage wasn't even on my mind. I was aware of this even when I married my first wife, who

5

was 12 years older than I and could not have any more children. I was 25 years old when I married the first time and the marriage didn't last a year. I was 28 when I remarried and my new wife already had one child, who was eight years old when we married and she turned nine that same year. I warned my new wife when we got married that the Lord told me one day I would have twin daughters.

I am sure my wife wondered if something was wrong with me. Well, three years after we were married my wife became pregnant with our son. Before knowing we were going to have a boy, I wondered if this pregnancy could have been the twins God showed me when I was 15 years old. It turned out that there was only one baby and it was a boy. I thanked God for having a healthy child. We now had two children. I loved our eldest daughter so much that I adopted her when she was 12 years old. In 1994, my wife became pregnant again and she really started to spread. In my mind, I knew there had to more than one for my wife's stomach was larger than when she was pregnant with our son. Once again, we found there was only one child and it was a girl.

I was happy with the arrival of our third child but I wondered if I misunderstood what God told me about one day having twin girls. Both of our ideal number of children were three. We both came from families that had seven children. About a year after having our third child I thought the twins were not going to happen so I consulted with a doctor about getting a vasectomy. Shortly after getting a consultation for the vasectomy, we found out my wife was pregnant!

I was really surprised and in disbelief. My wife called me from work and told me. I thought she was just playing around. She worked at a hospital and got someone to run a test for her. I realized she was not playing and was really pregnant. I had just purchased a used luxury car. The car was big enough for all of us including one more child. Two weeks later my wife was having stomach pain and we decided to go to the doctor. They sent us to a specialist who decided to do an ultrasound to see what was going on. The doctor asked us if we were on any fertility medicine. My wife broke out in tears for she knew what this meant. The doctor told us we had twins and the quick stomach expansion was what caused my wife pain. My wife and I were having a discussion after the news and she said she wanted to have a boy and a girl. I proclaimed to her that this was the twins God promised me so many years ago and I had no doubt they would be girls. I turned out to be true. When God promises something, we must remember He does things on His own time and schedule, not ours.

1 Timothy 6:11 tells us that people of God should "run from all these evil things. Pursue righteousness and a godly life, along with faith, love, perseverance, and gentleness. 1 Timothy 6:12 tells us to "Fight the good fight for the true faith. Hold tightly to the eternal life to which God has called you…"

As I just said, when my wife found out she was pregnant on her last pregnancy, we did not know she was pregnant with twins. They later determined her to be a high risk. We chose a method where she had to see an ultrasound specialist often to monitor the twins. That doctor later introduced us to another specialist who said due to my wife's risk factor, they thought it best if they conducted an amino synthesis test on her. My sister had one of those tests with her last pregnancy and, in my opinion, caused her problems that caused her to have her baby prematurely.

We prayed about this and The Lord showed me this test was not necessary. The specialist told us our twins may have problems if we did not have the test done. There I was telling two doctors that we will not have this test done for God told me it was not necessary. One doctor saw my point but the other one insisted. We left the office with my telling them I would not allow the test. One doctor continued to call my wife at home trying to convince her to take the test. I was still in the military as a middle-grade enlisted member and I had to call a medical officer and tell him to stop calling my wife for we had made our decision.

My wife made it far enough into the pregnancy that they said they needed to induce labor for the twins were getting too big to have a normal delivery. When our twins were born, the one persistent doctor came to the delivery and saw for himself our twins were fine, despite what he thought. I feel God uses doctors the help heal us but I also believe doctors don't know everything and God knows best!

Faith Through Bewilderment

In 1999 I was working happily at my job at MacDill AFB, FL when I began to feel it was time for me to retire. I prayed about it but did not feel I got an answer from the Lord. I then received a notification of a future change of station to the Pentagon. This meant I was doing a good job and I was being groomed for the next promotion; however, I felt more so that it was time for me to retire so I put in my retirement paperwork and started looking for a job. My retirement was set for May 2000.

As I looked for a job I wondered where to relocate my family. I got some promising potential for jobs in Florida and was closed to being accepted at the Largo, FL police department. That was the only fully committed to hiring job I had then one day the Lord spoke to me and told me not to accept the position with Largo PD. It wasn't that Largo PD was bad, don't get me wrong, it was that I felt the Lord had something else for me but I didn't know what it was. When I told people I was retiring but didn't have a job, they thought I was crazy. They wondered why I would turn down a job when I didn't have another one to go to.

This is when I felt God led to me to decide that I should move my family back to San Antonio, TX, where we had a house we were renting out to others. This made my decision to move back to San Antonio easier but I still wondered where I could find a job. My mind was made up for I knew what God had placed on my heart to do. You too should understand that some of the things God is leading you to do may seem impossible to you but nothing is impossible for God!

It wasn't until the movers were packing up our household goods that I got a call from the personnel office at my headquarters. They said they had reviewed my application package and wondered if I still wanted to come back to work as a civilian in my organization. I was excited at the offer and then told them it would depend on the location of the job. Guess what! They said the job was in San Antonio! Hallelujah! Isn't God great?! At a time when I didn't know where I would work but with five kids I knew I needed a job, God came through. I don't think it was coincidence that the job was in the location God showed me I should move back to. That was truly God at work and He has continually shown me His Grace since then.

Sometimes God blesses you in ways you never think of. Many times God will call on you to step out of your comfort zones and do things you never thought you were capable of doing. One such event happened to me and my family in 2003. In 2003, my family and I were happily living in our home in San Antonio, TX after I had retired from the military but worked for my organization as a civilian. My organization was going through some more changes which meant I had to move again.

Even though I didn't want to move for we had made some nice changes to our house in San Antonio to include building a custom shed and an above-ground pool in the back yard. My organization was trying to move me laterally under the same paygrade I was at my job in San Antonio. I thought this wasn't fair since I'd done a good job there and deserved a promotion. I went to my commander who agreed with me and he made some phone calls. I was given a promotion and a new position at Langley Air Force Base (AFB), VA.

My wife and I prayed about the move to Virginia. We were quite happy with our home in San Antonio but realized the promotion was a chance for me to advance in my career. We looked online and we both found a house that we really liked. We booked a house hunting trip so we could go see the house and check out the community. The problem was when we got there we found out that the house we wanted was only a plan and it had not been built yet! It was a disappointment to find it would take five to six months to build the house and we only had two months before we moved. I did not want to live in an apartment for six months with four kids (our eldest had moved out by then) while waiting for a house to be built.

We had our realtor show us some other homes Newport News and Hampton, VA. We liked some but did not like others. We wondered why the Lord would allow us to find something online we liked but it wasn't available when we got there. We expressed our dismay with our realtor who decided to take us to a new community in Williamsburg, VA that had a sold, but unoccupied new house like the one we wanted so we could see what it would look like. We loved the house! The only difference was this one had a crawl space under the house whereas the one we wanted was on a concrete slab.

As we were leaving the community we stopped by the builder's office on the premises and they told us that the persons who contracted on the house we looked at dropped out of the contract for personal reasons the night before and they were just getting ready to put the house on the market again but at a higher price. We told them there was no need to do that for we would buy the house for it was just what we were looking for. God made a way for us when there seemed to be no other way! We put a contract on the house and it was ready for us when we moved there. God is so faithful!

In 2005, my family and I were living comfortably in Williamsburg, VA. We loved our community but my wife hated being in Virginia. She told me she would stay in Virginia with me for only three years. At that time, we had been there for two years. My mother became ill and I had made a few trips to Atlanta to visit her. I had come to the realization that when my mother got out of the hospital, she would not be as independent as she had previously been. On the last trip to Atlanta, my family stayed in Virginia and I drove alone and stayed with my older brother, who lived in Fayetteville, GA. He and his new wife had just built a nice home there. My visit with my mother went well but she was still in the hospital when I left going back to Virginia. That morning I prayed like I usually do and got into my 2004 Toyota Prius. I had just left my brother's house and something told me to stop and look at a house being built that I have never noticed before. The house was in my brother's community and there were other houses being built and a few were recently completed. This may be a familiar story to some of you.

The house was being framed and you could not really tell how it was going to look. I immediately took my video camera out and started filming. The realtor and builder just happen to be at the house that day and I found out there were a few builders in the community and this builder was building this house as his first home that would serve as his model. The realtor was nice and answered my questions. He confirmed that that house was going to be a model but the builder might consider selling it. The words and questions that came out of my mouth astonished me. I asked the realtor, how many bedrooms does "my" house have? I also asked, how much land does "my" house sit on? I then said to the realtor, listen to me talk as if I owned the house and I wasn't even in the market for a home.

I really liked the house even though at that time I had not seen any photos or plans on how the house was supposed to look, I just knew in my spirit that God told me this was going to be my house and it was being built for my family and I. I even loved how the house sat in the community and there was only one other house that would be near me. The other side had a green space and a creek running through. The realtor told me the plan name for the house and I could look up what the house would look like on the Internet. I called my wife excited about what I had found even though I did not understand why I was looking at a house.

As I drove on home and was traveling up I-85 I keep praying to the Lord about what all this meant for there was no intention for my job with the government to move me and I didn't have money to place on this new house. I said Lord, please show me what's going on. Then I got a phone call on my cell phone. It was my boss informing me that I had been selected to deploy to Iraq. I knew I had no choice but to go or quit my job. Now I knew what was going on for God knew that if I had deployed while my wife and family were in Virginia, she would have left me. To my surprise, she immediately agreed to work with me on moving to Fayetteville, GA.

My mother ended up getting sick again so the family and I got to travel back to Atlanta. We stayed with my brother again and the whole family got the see the house I intended to purchase. The house had taken on more shape now and you could get a better idea of what it would look like when finished. My wife and children liked the house but saw other nice houses in the neighborhood that were already available. My wife asked me to buy a nice house up the street from the one we were looking. I told her no for God had already showed me the house we would purchase and I would never go against His will. We stood in what I called the second driveway to my house (an access road) and I

16

declared to my family that if this house was for us, which I knew it was, then God would have something in the mail when we got back to Virginia that would help us put earnest money on this house. Guess what, there was a check in the mail when we got home that did just that!

The pending deployment became my second reason for moving to Atlanta. Being on the south side of Atlanta made it easy for my wife to travel to see her family in Florida. My first reason for wanting to move was so my mother could eventually live with us. I wanted to make sure she was being taken care of. Unfortunately, after we started the process of buying the house by putting money down and signing a contract, my mother passed away. This really threw me for a loop! Now, my primary reason for moving home was gone.

I realized I had to stay the course on the move for my wife was ready to leave Virginia. On one hand the community we lived in was great! Nice location, beautiful home, and wonderful neighbors. But I knew all that would not matter if my wife was left there alone with the kids while I was in Iraq. On the other hand, the situation on my job had become deplorable! For the first time in my job history, I hated going to work. The backstabbing and lies was getting to me. The backstabbing was what caused me to have to deploy. This became more obvious when I told them what I was going through as I started preparing to bury my mother.

I had to fall on my face in prayer asking the Lord what was going on. I knew the Lord led me to purchase the home we were building and I thought it was mainly so my mother could live with us. Now I had trouble understanding why God would allow my mother to pass in the middle of my coming home. Through prayer, God allowed me to understand He was still in control even though I did not understand what was going on. I wondered what I should do and where could I turn to face the multiple problems I faced. I had to realize there is power in the name of Jesus! I cried out to the Lord for help.

At that time, it seemed like my problems became bigger. I was getting ready to bury my mother, the house in Williamsburg had not sold, the deployment to Iraq was still looming, and my organization would not give me a transfer to Atlanta. The problem became worse when I asked my organization to cancel my deployment for I knew that dealing with the sadness of losing my mother and having to take care of personal matters after burying her had become too much to handle. I told my leadership it wasn't that I wouldn't deploy, it was just that I wanted to put it off to a later time. They were relentless that I go now.

This all came to head after I took bereavement leave from work to attend my mother's funeral. My leadership knew I was going home to bury my mother but nothing had changed. I was told I still had to deploy to Iraq. The only other option I had was to refuse to go, which would allow them to start the process to fire me for my position required me to be available to deploy if needed. My commander told me I had to make a decision. On the day of my mother's funeral, my commander called me and asked me what my decision was. I told him respectfully that I was getting ready to bury my mother that day and I will not make the trip to Iraq. He asked me if I knew what that meant and I told him yes. He said he would meet with me when I returned to work. My back was against the wall and all I could do was to turn to the Lord and tell Him this situation was in His hands and I needed help.

My mother's funeral went well and she had a nice send off to heaven. I enjoyed seeing my family, many of whom I hadn't seen in many years. I knew I had to face the music with my job when I got back to Virginia. This is when I began to see the light in my situation and knew God was on my side. No matter how bad things looked, I had to put my trust in Him. I knew the meeting with my commander was going to be tough when he invited his deputy to sit in the meeting with us. Before I got there, I asked the Lord to guide my tongue and my actions during the meeting. My commander essentially said that since I choose not to deploy, it meant I was either tendering my resignation or face being fired. I told him I would not resign. He asked me didn't I say I understood what it meant when I told him that I would not deploy. I told him yes that under normal circumstances it meant that I could be fired. I told him this circumstance was different in that I was not refusing to ever deploy but turned down the deployment for I asked how could I be focused to protect myself and the people that worked with me I if was distracted with personal issues.

My commander insisted on putting words in my mouth that I didn't say. His own witness confirmed that. He told me he had a war to fight and my personal issues was not a priority. He said I would either have to take the deployment still or face being fired. I told him that as a man, father, and husband I had to do what was best for my family and I would not go to Iraq at that time; however, I would not resign. I left the meeting frustrated though confident that God would deliver me. I asked the Lord what I needed to do since it was apparent things were not in my favor at that moment. I was not a political person that dropped names of who I knew to get people to respond to what I wanted. The Lord led me to make a phone call to someone I knew and explain the situation. That person was the second in command of my entire organization. I told him my situation and explained I wasn't implying that I would never deploy but given the personal crisis I faced, I wanted them to stop the current deployment.

My commander called me to another meeting the next day. He looked stunned! He told me he did not know I knew the deputy to the commander. The deputy to the commander called him at home the night before and told him to "leave Freddy Wilson alone". The deputy to the commander knew I was a man of my word and had good reasons to not deploy at that moment. He was confident that I would deploy if circumstances did not prevent me from going. My commander cancelled my deployment. I was truly relieved for I knew the next couple of months would be stressful. God is so good! What was strange about this was that within a month of my being taken off the Iraq deployment, I was selected to deploy to Afghanistan but at a later date. I don't know what the motive was behind this but I was sure that it was a test to see what I would do, and possibly an attempt to force me to resign. I wasn't concerned for I knew God would bless me and my family.

I believe being selected to deploy to Afghanistan was set up to destroy me but it ended up being a blessing. My wife, son, and I, packed a self-move using three large PODS, a large rental trailer, and a separate trip in a rented pickup truck from a 3,000 square foot home. It was a lot of work but we were able to pull it off. The deployment provided me experience in areas I had never experienced before, I met new friends, and built my faith and alliance with God. The money I made on the deployment paid for some improvements in the home we purchased and paid for a nice vacation when I came back from Afghanistan. The same commander that once persecuted me became a blessing for he approved an assignment to Atlanta after I returned from deployment. To top it all off, the government paid for my move after the fact! I again loved going to work at my new location. God is truly amazing!

The Storms of Life

The Bible speaks to us about the storms in life. The storms in life are any kinds of trouble, difficulty, or physical and mental distresses that we may face. The Bible says this storm will pass. It simply means that all storms come to an end. When you're trying to live your life right, the devil will sometimes try to make you regret doing the right thing. I've learned that being in a storm is indication you are heading in the right direction. How you handle your storm is key to your success!

Sometimes God will allow you to enter into a storm just to make you stronger. The greater your storm, the greater your destiny, purpose, or blessing. You should learn to be at peace when you're going through a storm. We are all human so thinking about different issues and wondering how to handle them is normal. However, if you have faith in God, you can put your worries aside! Remember, Jesus rested during the storm in one of the Bible stories.

You should rest during your storms. Rest during your storms and have faith in God that He will bring you through them. Your faith should tell you that 'this too shall pass'. When you become more blessed you should never put your trust in your money or your talents. 1 Timothy 6:17-19 tells us to, "Teach those who are rich in this world not to be proud and not to trust in their money, which is so unreliable. Their trust should be in God, who richly gives us all we need for our enjoyment. Tell them to use their money to do good. They should be rich in good works and generous to those in need, always being ready to share with others. By doing this they will be storing up their treasure as a good foundation for the future so that they may experience true life."

Some of you need to have a life changing encounter. One example of a life changing encounter is the story of when Jesus met the Samaritan woman at the well. John 4:11-24 discusses this:

The Samaritan woman said, [11]"But sir, you don't have a rope or a bucket," she said, "and this well is very deep. Where would you get this living water? Jesus told the woman [13] "Anyone who drinks this water will soon become thirsty again. [14]But those who drink the water I give will never be thirsty again. It becomes a fresh, bubbling spring within them, giving them eternal life." The discussion went on and the woman started questioning about the proper place for them to worship God. Jesus explained, [23]But the time is coming—indeed it's here now—when true worshipers will worship the Father in spirit and in truth.

The Father is looking for those who will worship him that way. [24]For God is Spirit, so those who worship him must worship in spirit and in truth."

One point of this story is that shame will make you do unusual things. The woman felt ashamed she was not aware of the power of Jesus' spirit. Also, Jesus' meeting with the woman was not happenchance. Jesus made it purposeful even though the woman was not aware. You need to have your own encounter with the Lord. Go to the Lord without condition. It doesn't matter the place that we go to the Lord, whether it at our homes, workplaces, or church. We should not want salvation on our own terms. We need to make a change and stop doing things only the way we think they should be done, even it's the traditions we are so used to.

Jesus intensified the encounter by confronting the woman about husbands she didn't have. The woman was in awe for she thought her lifestyle was a secret only to the men she dealt with. A point of grace here is that Jesus did not condemn the woman but corrected her. The first six men the woman met wanted to lay the woman down, Jesus (the seventh) wanted to lift her up. We all need uplifting moments with Jesus in our lives.

Religion normally indicate we get salvation and the Word of God only in houses of worship. The truth is, you can worship God anywhere. It's not where you worship, but who you worship. God Almighty is the only one true God. God is spirit and must be worshipped in spirit and in truth. Another good thing about this encounter with Jesus was that the woman went out and told others about Jesus. John 4:28 said, "²⁸ The woman left her water jar beside the well and ran back to the village, telling everyone."

A Call to Repentance

We must repent from the sinful things of our past. Once we do, God has a plan to prosper us! We can start by learning how to pay our tithes. Malachi 3:10 calls for us to, "bring all the tithes into the storehouse so there will be enough food in my Temple." God showed us in Malachi that if you do, he "will pour out a blessing so great you won't have enough room to take it in!" Malachi tells us we can put God to the test.

Psalms 126:3 said the LORD has done amazing things for us! Many times, God blesses us whether we believe or not for He is just being God and providing for all people. At other times God blesses us for being obedient to His directions and principles. We must have faith that God will provide for us. Hebrews 11:1 said faith is being sure of what we hope for and being convinced of what we do not see. Hebrews 11:6 (NET) says, "without faith it is impossible to please him, for the one who approaches God must believe that he exists and that he rewards those who seek him."

You may have heard the stories about my being deployed to Afghanistan in 2006 and to Iraq in 2009. Somehow my name came up again to deploy to Afghanistan in April 2013 and December 2013. I was tired of being selected when I knew there were many civilians in my job who had not deployed. Through my supervisor I told my HQ I did not want to go again and I definitely did not volunteer to deploy anywhere. I prayed to God that if there was no purpose in His Will for me not to go, then cancel anyone's thoughts about sending me. God blessed me not to have to go. This was due to me standing on God's Word and being bold to say no.

I pray to God daily. First thing I do when I wake up is get down on my knees and thank the Lord to seeing another day. I am constantly praying to God during the day and it's the last thing I do when I go to bed at night. This is how I began to understand that there are things in life we have to endure and trust God will bring us out. Just as I was working on paying off bad debt, bringing my credit score up, and things getting better financially, some creditors decided to write-off debts instead of giving me a chance to get caught up. As a result, in 2013 when I applied for loan for my son to attend summer classes, I was denied due to the charge-offs. I initially became distraught for my son worked too hard to bring his grades up and stay in school, I didn't want him to have to quit. God made a way! His grandmother co-signed to loan for us that period. I didn't want to involve anyone into our problems but sometimes you have to do unusual things to move forward in life.

In 2014, I was denied again for his loan and for our middle child, a daughter. However, this time when I applied for a waiver, the waiver was granted because my credit score had improved. I now don't have to request waivers and loan requests for all my children are approved the first time. This goes to show if you have faith and stay in the Will of God, there are rewards. Luke 5: 4-6 discusses order, doubt, and reward: "[4]When he had finished speaking, he said to Simon, 'Now go out where it is deeper, and let down your nets to catch some fish.' [5] 'Master,' Simon replied, 'we worked hard all last night and didn't catch a thing. But if you say so, I'll let the nets down again.' [6]And this time their nets were so full of fish they began to tear!"

We have to stand in the blood of Jesus to progress successfully in life. The truth about the blood is that it has everlasting power! In the midst of unsettling things that can happen in life, don't get distraught over it, it's not permanent! 2 Corinthians 4:8-9 says, "[8]We are pressed on every side by troubles, but we are not crushed. We are perplexed, but not driven to despair. [9]We are hunted down, but never abandoned by God." We get knocked down, but we are not destroyed.

The fact is, God has a plan for you. God will bless you through your problems. The problem is you don't learn as much in victory as you do in defeat. You have to learn you're not as in control of everything as you think you are. This is more so with financially successful people and those who are well-educated. If you trust God, He will take you to another level.

You must understand that problems are not to destroy you but to develop you. I suggest you continue to praise God throughout your problems. You should praise God not for what He has done for you but for who He is to you. Here's one for you: All your struggles are for your benefit! 2 Corinthians 4:15 says "15All of this is for your benefit. And as God's grace reaches more and more people, there will be great thanksgiving, and God will receive more and more glory." 2 Corinthians 4:16 says, do not lose heart. I'm saying all this to say, don't give up, and don't quit, for you are being renewed every day.

2 Corinthians 4:16 says, "16That is why we never give up. Though our bodies are dying, our spirits are being renewed every day. 2 Corinthians 4:17 says we are dealing with

momentary troubles: [17]For our present troubles are small and won't last very long. Yet they produce for us a glory that vastly outweighs them and will last forever!" Remember, our walk with Jesus is towards change, but we need to work!

Money and Possessions

Many people in the past have said the money is the route of all evil. I beg to differ, I think the lack of money is the route of all evil! Don't get me wrong. There are many people who have money and have done wrong with it and for it. There's nothing wrong with having money. It's just not something we should worship.

Matthew 6:19 - 21 tells us, "[19]Don't store up treasures here on earth, where moths eat them and rust destroys them, and where thieves break in and steal. [20]Store your treasures in heaven, where moths and rust cannot destroy, and thieves do not break in and steal. [21]Wherever your treasure is, there the desires of your heart will also be." You should never treasure money over your relationship with God and others.

You have to make up your mind as to how you are going to represent God's light in you. At the Sermon on the Mount, some of the disciples wanted to be led, while others wanted to just be in the crowd. Matthew 5:1-2 says, "[1]One day as he saw the crowds gathering, Jesus went up on the mountainside and sat down. His disciples gathered around him, [2]and he began to teach them." You have to be able to control your flesh if you want to be blessed. If you can't control your flesh, you are delaying your blessings.

Jesus was never interested in gaining money. He had money but was not focused on it. Jesus spent his time doing for others. What have you done with your talent or your money for others? You should seek to help others and God will bless you.

You should consider this your "Do" Season. Psalms 34:10 tells us, "^{10} Even strong young lions sometimes go hungry, but those who trust in the LORD will lack no good thing." It's time for us to do something. We can no longer sit back and watch the world go by and not get involved. We should be openly willingly to share the Word of God with others. What are you doing to show God your passion for Him? What are you doing to prepare yourself for your new season? If you are seeking God, what are you doing?

You have to have a "striving" and not a "surviving" mentality. You say you don't have enough time in your life to do something great for God? God can give you more time to spend with your family, showing your gifts, etc. You have to speak the fact that you will prosper! You can't stay where you are and expect a blessing, you have to do something! You got to have faith, you must trust and praise God. Matthew 6:33 says to, "^{33}Seek the Kingdom of God above all else, and live righteously, and he will give you everything you need."

You should not be ashamed of having a positive, God-blessed attitude! You should never tire of doing what is right even when everyone around you are doing the wrong things. Galatians 6:9 says, "^{9}So let's not get tired of doing what is good." At just the right time we will reap a harvest of blessing if we don't give up. You have to continually do the following: 1) stock up for success, 2) schedule for your success, 3) share your success, and 4) build on your success. All you have to do during these processes is lean on God.

Throughout times that you're trying to progress there will be storms you have to go through. The storms should produce life. You can count on God to calm you during the storms. Mark 4:35-40 tells us how Jesus calmed the storm. Mark 4:35 - 40 says, "[35]As evening came, Jesus said to his disciples, 'Let's cross to the other side of the lake.' [36]So they took Jesus in the boat and started out, leaving the crowds behind (although other boats followed). [37]But soon a fierce storm came up. High waves were breaking into the boat, and it began to fill with water. [38]Jesus was sleeping at the back of the boat with his head on a cushion. The disciples woke him up, shouting, 'Teacher, don't you care that we're going to drown?' [39]When Jesus woke up, he rebuked the wind and said to the water, 'Silence! Be still!' Suddenly the wind stopped, and there was a great calm. [40]Then he asked them, 'Why are you afraid? Do you still have no faith?'"

We all become weak while going through storms. Having faith in God will give you strength to endure. Not only should the storm produce life for you, your storm should produce life for someone else. After Jesus calmed the storm in his disciples' lives, he went on to help someone else. Mark 5:1-4 tells us how Jesus healed a demon-possessed man. Mark 5:1-4 reads, "[1]So they arrived at the other side of the lake, in the region of the Gerasenes. ²When Jesus climbed out of the boat, a man possessed by an evil spirit came out from a cemetery to meet him. ³This man lived among the burial caves and could no longer be restrained, even with a chain. ⁴Whenever he was put into chains and shackles—as he often was—he snapped the chains from his wrists and smashed the shackles. No one was strong enough to subdue him."

Even though this man was not a part of Jesus' group he saw a need and got involved. If it had not been for Jesus, where would we be? You are allowed to get through storms so you can be a blessing to someone else. Your testimony is important so you can let someone else know how God brought you through. Don't forget where you came from. Let someone else know.

There are things to be careful of as you go through storms. During tough times, guard your heart against negativity. You have to remain faithful. Did you know that on the other side of pain is greatness? I suggest you continually speak life and blessings in all things. Proverbs 18:21 says, "²¹The tongue can bring death or life; those who love to talk will reap the consequences." Always trust God and speak a positive word into your life and circumstances!

How to Deal with Your Enemies

We must be careful when dealing with our enemies. By no means am I suggesting we run from our enemies but we must look at our enemies differently. Sometimes God works through our enemies to get us to where He needs us to be. 1 Samuel 24 tells the story of how David could have killed Saul. Our desires with our enemies should not be one of revenge. King Saul had his men looking for David to kill him. David and his men were hiding in a cave where Saul went to relieve himself. David was physically very close to Saul but Saul was unaware that David could have killed him. This is what David said to Saul after not killing him when he had a chance: 1 Samuel 24:15 says, "[15]May the LORD therefore judge which of us is right and punish the guilty one. He is my advocate, and he will rescue me from your power!"

David's soldiers told him to kill Saul since Saul wanted to kill David. David was much wiser than that. We must watch the advice we follow. The advice we follow must line up with God's Word. There are blessings with having a sensitive conscious. David's conscience kept him from killing Saul. Passages in Romans showed David spoke the word of God to his men. Romans 12:14-19 reads, "[14]Bless those who persecute you. Don't curse them; pray that God will bless them. [15]Be happy with those who are happy, and weep with those who weep. [16]Live in harmony with each other. Don't be too proud to enjoy the company of ordinary people. And don't think you know it all! [17]Never pay back evil with more evil. Do things in such a way that everyone can see you are honorable. [18]Do all that you can to live in peace with everyone. [19]Dear friends, never take revenge. Leave that to the righteous anger of God. For the Scriptures say, 'I will take revenge; I will pay them back,' says the LORD."

David repaid Saul for his actions with love and promised not to kill Saul's family when David becomes king. David knew that God would deal with David's enemies. In fact, David's actions caused Saul shame by showing him love at a time when most men would have shown hatred. When we love our enemies, we are behaving like our father in heaven.

All believers have great potential inside them. Great potential must be mothered before it can flourish.

1 Corinthians 4:14 - 15 says, "[14]I am not writing these things to shame you, but to warn you as my beloved children. [15]For even if you had ten thousand others to teach

you about Christ, you have only one spiritual father. For I became your father in Christ Jesus when I preached the Good News to you." At my church in Tampa, FL we talked about the father void. We live in a world where the father is absent or not involved. In a good family, the father is always there for his family. In a Godly sense, the blessing always flows down from the Father! There is a God sized solution for every one of our man-sized problems! You should find the Father and be a father! The bible describes God as a Father 220 times! You should allow God to heal the father wound in your life.

The Power of Prayer

Most of what I'm talking about is accomplished through prayer. James 5:16 tells us, "[16]Confess your sins to each other and pray for each other so that you may be healed. The earnest prayer of a righteous person has great power and produces wonderful results." Don't make it a secret that you're praying about your problems. You will stay sick as long as you stay secret!

Many people want to show the world how "religious" they are by going to church and displaying Bibles in their homes. You should look for something more fulfilling by developing a personal relationship with God. Your greatest fulfillment will be found moving past religion and to a real relationship with God! James 1:17 - 18 says, "[17]Whatever is good and perfect comes down to us from God our Father, who created all the lights in the heavens. He never changes or casts a shifting shadow. [18]He chose to give birth to us by giving us his true word. And we, out of all creation, became his prized possession."

Your communications with God should be face-to-face, shoulder-to-shoulder, and back to back. This will keep you secure while facing the problems in life. You should realize that struggles in life is proof you're not defeated.

Ephesians 6:10-12 reads, "[10]A final word: Be strong in the Lord and in his mighty power. [11]Put on all of God's armor so that you will be able to stand firm against all strategies of the devil. [12]For we are not fighting against flesh-and-blood enemies, but against evil rulers and authorities of the unseen world, against mighty powers in this dark world, and against evil spirits in the heavenly places." Ephesians 6:18 tells us, "[18]Pray in the Spirit at all times and on every occasion." Stay alert and be persistent in your prayers for all believers everywhere.

When you become a Christian, it doesn't mean all your problems are over and you'll never experience any problems in your life. Being a Christian means you will have victory over the problems you face. One thing you must understand as a Christian is that the devil wants to attack your mind. Symptoms of a mind under attack - flashing thoughts, lack of sleep, lack of concentration, and double mindedness. To thwart attacks on your mind I recommend you get in the Word and pray in the Spirit.

You may sometimes find yourself getting angry when dealing with problems. The problem is not the anger itself but losing control. You should never lose control of your emotions. This only leads to problems or disaster. In the book of Matthew there is a story where Simon Peter was talking to Jesus. Matthew 16:17 tells us, "[17]Jesus replied, "You are blessed, Simon son of John, because my

Father in heaven has revealed this to you. You did not learn this from any human being."

Just when you think that you're dead in the middle of your crisis, you can be made alive in Christ. Ephesians 2:1 tells us, "¹Once you were dead because of your disobedience and your many sins." You need to stand up and fight for your freedom. At other times you need to let the Lord fight your battles. You need to allow God to fight your battles. Exodus 17:8-13 tells the story of Joshua allowing the Lord to fight his battles:

Exodus 17:8 - 13 (NLT) ⁸While the people of Israel were still at Rephidim, the warriors of Amalek attacked them. ⁹Moses commanded Joshua, "Choose some men to go out and fight the army of Amalek for us. Tomorrow, I will stand at the top of the hill, holding the staff of God in my hand." ¹⁰So Joshua did what Moses had commanded and fought the army of Amalek. Meanwhile, Moses, Aaron, and Hur climbed to the top of a nearby hill. ¹¹As long as Moses held up the staff in his hand, the Israelites had the advantage. But whenever he dropped his hand, the Amalekites gained the advantage. ¹²Moses' arms soon became so tired he could no longer hold them up. So Aaron and Hur found a stone for him to sit on. Then they stood on each side of Moses, holding up his hands. So his hands held steady until sunset. ¹³As a result, Joshua overwhelmed the army of Amalek in battle.

You must understand you'll never outgrow spiritual warfare. The devil does not want to see you at peace. Spiritual warfare surrounds the birth of a miracle. Remain faithful and don't let anyone or anything shake your faith in God. You'll find that a hindering spirit is a lying spirit. Never say anything to let the devil know he's winning. The older you get in the Lord, the more intense your battles will be.

Those that love the Lord should want justice for themselves and others. If you don't want justice, you don't want Jesus. Matthew 5:17 - 18 tells us, "[17]Don't misunderstand why I have come. I did not come to abolish the law of Moses or the writings of the prophets. No, I came to accomplish their purpose. [18]I tell you the truth, until heaven and earth disappear, not even the smallest detail of God's law will disappear until its purpose is achieved."

To succeed you must start living in the Faith Zone. Your family should be important to you, so get it together! Faith is important in dealing with everyday life. Seeking God's Will produces favor in your life. This favor will take your farther than you can ever imagine. Jesus' healing a demon-possessed boy in Mark 9:22 shows us all things are possible. Mark 9:23 tells us, "Anything is possible if a person believes."

The Bible continually tells us how we need to have faith in God. Hebrews 11:6 reads, "⁶And it is impossible to please God without faith." Anyone who wants to come to him must believe that God exists and that he rewards those who sincerely seek him. If you only knew the power of God, there will be no doubt of what He's capable of doing for you. Hebrews 12:27 says, "This means that all of creation will be shaken and removed, so that only unshakable things will remain."

Having faith is the key to breakthrough. The passages in Mark 4:38-40 shows us we have to break out of our circumstances and needless worry. Jesus calmed the storm faced by his disciples and he can calm the storms in your life. In Mark 4:40, Jesus asked his disciples, "Why are you afraid? Do you still have no faith?" You have to break out of fear, your past, and negative thinking! Three simple ways to do this: 1) start where you are, 2) Use what you have, and 3) Do what you can. You just can't sit there and wait for something to happen, you have to press your way!!

You've heard before you should never let anyone steal your joy. When you find the Lord, you find joy. There is strength in joy. With joy you can always say, I'm too blessed to be stressed! You must maintain a positive outlook on negative situations. Let your joy help you stay encouraged. Acts 20:25 tells you to finish your course. Tell yourself, "I shall finish my course with joy!" John 14:1 says to let not your heart be troubled.

When you have a relationship with God, you should be willing to obey Him. This should come not as a matter of fear but one of reverence, love, and respect. Deuteronomy 11:26, 27, 28 discusses obeying God. You should obey God even if you don't feel like doing it! You can't do anything pertaining to God outside of God. You can obey God by simply yielding to His Word. The first avenue God will use to get you to obey is His Word. You can find the Word of God in the Bible.

Every act of obedience moves you towards His Will. No one can determine what God wants you to do, others can confirm it, but only God can determine it. One act of obedience leads you to the next act of obedience. The hardest task you do for God will bring about the greatest blessing. You can read more about this in 1 Samuel.

One thing I encourage you to do is to not settle for less than what God has for you. Don't settle in anything you do! Passages in Genesis shows us how we can see it's easy to get out of faith. Sometimes we try to put our plan into action for God. You can't outdo God! Don't put too much faith in your money, your skills, your abilities, and station in life. Don't ever compromise with the devil. When you compromise with the devil, you always end up tricked. Psalms 27 tells us to wait on the Lord. Stay in faith!

We must not act out of the flesh. There are three characters of the flesh: 1) It settles; 2) It's limited to the physical. God's ability is supernatural so He can go beyond the natural. Things of the flesh are done by what's natural, normal, and often depends on numbers; 3) the flesh settles for the immediate. This is normally something that is below standards. Hebrews 10:36 tells us to have patience. Romans 8:9 says, "But you are not controlled by your sinful nature. You are controlled by the Spirit if you have the Spirit of God living in you. (And remember that those who do not have the Spirit of Christ living in them do not belong to him at all.)"

God's purpose is never static. To live on past glory is to miss present action. Hebrews 3:25 tells us that Jesus prays for us. Did you know that Jesus is the ruler of God's earth? Jesus is the radiance of God. Jesus is also God's revealer. Colossians 1:27 tells us that Christ is in us. Jesus is the regent of God's power. With this we have no reason to fear anything or anyone we face. 2 Tim 1:7 said God has not given us the spirit of fear. Philippians 4:13-14 says, "For I can do everything through Christ, who gives me strength. Even so, you have done well to share with me in my present difficulty."

Jesus is redeemer of God's people and the recipient of God's honor. All we have to do is look to Jesus to find the answer to our problems. We honor God by coming to Him first with our problems. After all, He already knows what we are going through. Sometimes our issue is that we are not fully using the gifts God gives each us. You must honor God with your gifts. It's time for you to use what you have to honor God.

What can God use that you have to help others to Christ? All Peter had to offer the lame man was Jesus. It's not about you but the God within you. Just look and see what God is doing in your life. Talk is cheap, put faith in action! There's power in the name of Jesus. Don't focus on what

you don't have. What you do have is the name of Jesus.
Philippians 4:19 says, "And this same God who takes care
of me will supply all your needs from his glorious riches,
which have been given to us in Christ Jesus."

What some people don't understand is that even if you
don't believe in God, He believes in you and blesses even
the non-believers. I believe the believers have more power
to conquer problems in their lives. With God you can take
It or leave It! God will keep you even when you don't
want to be kept.

We have to make conscience decisions to follow Christ.
There are consequences to decisions we make in our walk
with Christ. Take your troubles to Jesus and leave them
there! You must let your problems go! You should
continue to go to church and worship the Lord regardless of
your problems. Have you ever asked yourself, what brings
you to church? It's that fellowship you need. It's
important to give but you can't throw money at your
problems. Christians must be able to stand on their own
two feet and step out on faith in God. You have to come to
the Lord's house with an expectation for a blessing. What
happens when God does not give you what you want, but
what you need? God knows what's best for you.

You have to have the audacity to dream! Dreaming with audacity is a gift from God. Your blessings are in your ability to dream. You must trust that God will deliver on his promises. But you must rest in his Word. Hebrews 4:3 says, "For only we who believe can enter his rest. As for the others, God said, "In my anger I took an oath: 'They will never enter my place of rest,'" even though this rest has been ready since he made the world. With faith, the place we can't see is more real that the place you can see.

The season is now for kingdom of God to be released! Don't despise the challenges and tests you'll have. It's necessary to build your character and faith that will make you grow stronger in the Lord. 1 Peter 2:9 says, "But you are not like that, for you are a chosen people. You are royal priests, a holy nation, God's very own possession. As a result, you can show others the goodness of God, for he called you out of the darkness into his wonderful light."

There are barriers to breakthroughs:

1. Getting over loneliness. You may be by yourself, but with God you're never alone!

2. Getting over long hurts. Let's face it, people will hurt you. The sooner you forgive them and move on, the sooner you'll get better.

3. Continuous disappointment. Some disappointing things happen to us as we live our lives. If we face them with the attitude that all is not over, you can get past the disappointments. Some disappointments have purposes.

4. Thinking you don't have what it takes to deal with problems. If you have God, you have what it takes to tackle any problem that comes your way.

You have to be willing to seek the Lord. No one can force you to get in touch with the Master. The story in the Bible about the woman with an issue of blood is an example of letting nothing stop you from getting to the Lord. That woman had faith. Any suffering you're dealing with must be spoken to in order to be broken. Jesus heals the hurts in our lives. 1 Peter 5:10 says, "In his kindness God called you to share in his eternal glory by means of Christ Jesus. So after you have suffered a little while, he will restore, support, and strengthen you, and he will place you on a firm foundation."

You must be obedient and do what God will have you do. You must sometimes gather with like-minded people and pray together. There is strength in prayer when you bind with others! Matthew 18:19 says, "I also tell you this: If two of you agree here on earth concerning anything you ask, my Father in heaven will do it for you." There a saying about no man being an island unto himself. That applies to the social realm as well as the spiritual realm. Ask friends and associates to pray for you and your family.

You should keep looking for your final breakthrough. Your breakthrough may come from the most unlikely sources and from the most unlikely people. The story told in Mark 5:21-34 about the woman who touched the garment of Jesus is but one example. Jesus had got into a boat and went to the other side of the lake where a crowd had gathered. A leader of a local synagogue directed Jesus to his daughter who was dying. There was a woman in the crowd who had suffered for twelve years with constant bleeding. No one could help her, not even the doctors. The woman thought to herself, "If I can just touch his robe, I will be healed." When worked her way through the crowd and touched Jesus' garment, the bleeding stopped immediately, and she could feel in her body that she had been healed. Jesus told the woman that her faith made her well. This was definitely an uncommon blessing in the common way they approached problems at that time. You too should apply your faith at every opportunity to address your wounds and problems. Allow the uncommon blessings to find your common problems.

Don't Tie God's Hands

We really need to watch how we pray. Before the Lord blessed us to close on our Tampa Townhouse in July 2016, I asked my apartment complex if it would be alright for me to break my lease. I had been living in these apartments for 2-1/2 years and always paid my rent on time. One of the clerks told me there won't be a problem. When I later announced that I would be moving out but I couldn't give them a date of move put, again I was told that won't be a problem.

A little later on and when I went in and gave them a move out date, I was again told by one of the clerks my moving out won't be a problem and there wouldn't be a penalty. After my apartment passed inspection, we went and turned in our keys. The manager was there and said there won't be a problem and I can expect to see my deposit within the next week. My wife was with me and witnessed the manager tell me everything was fine.

One week after we moved into our new townhome, I got a registered letter from my former apartment complex indicating I owed them $2,011.00 for breaking my lease! I was outraged! I contacted the apartment manager and told her the story of how things went and told her she said everything was fine. This is when she told me that at the time she told me this, she had not read my lease. That was not my fault! All the time I was telling them my situation, she should have read the lease. I explained that I knew what the lease said but I left based on the idea they supported that I would not have to pay a penalty.

I later wrote them a letter asking for reconsideration and she held fast. I said to God, Lord bless me to not have to pay this fee but they said I had to pay it. Again, I had to realize that I should not tie God's hands by telling Him how to bless me. Then I prayed that God makes a way for me to pay this bill. If I had agreed to pay them at the beginning (July 2016), then I would have paid them off by October, but I didn't have the money. On 31 October 2016, I signed a promissory note for the balance ($2022.00) and wrote them a check for $100.00, dated 1 November 2016. The blessing at this time was being able to hold them at bay until I had some breathing room to save some money.

My prayer was that my old apartment complex would not charge me this early termination fee. I realized later that I should have just prayed that God made a way for me in this situation. God had already blessed me to delay the apartment complex from collecting the money sooner. I then realized God can bless me with the money to pay this fee. I looked forward to God blessing me to pay this fee. I've learned many times along my life that if you stay in His Will, God will always make a way!

The next blessing was after I made that payment on 31 October 2016, they wanted to make the first full payment due in November 2016. I told them since we are almost already in November, I knew I could not have made another payment in November. They agreed in writing that my next payment would be due in December 2016 and the final payment would be due in February 2017. The caveat on this agreement was that each payment won't be past due until the end of the month in which it was due. This meant I would have to have paid the entire remaining $1922 by 28 February 2017. I still didn't know how I would do this considering I would then be paying two mortgages, one where my family lived in Georgia and the other on the new loan on our townhouse in Florida.

I prayed that God would show me how I would make these payments. God blessed me to be able the make these payments until 1 March 2017 when I was finally able to pay the balance in full. I knew God had blessed us with the new townhouse but I began to wonder how he would bless me to pay the money I owed. As far as I was concerned I should not have owed them anything. They had a better case if we went to court for it was written in the contract; however, when dealing with them directly, the early move-out fee was supposed to be waived. When people come against you, look to God for answers! I didn't have the resources to pay them but God first blessed me to delay the payments and then he blessed me with the resources to pay them off. The moral of the story is to stop telling God how to bless you! Pray and put your problems in his hands. Not only will He guide you, but He'll also give you the provisions you need.

Use Your Experience and Faith to Encourage Others

One of my twins came to me and said we needed to apply for another student loan for her 2016-2017 school year. I did so and was approved right away. She was proud to have gone to summer school and brought up her GPA. Sometimes crazy things happen as you move in God's Will. She called me frantic one day and said the school sent her a random verification we had to do. My daughter was worried for a friend of hers told her she had to go through the same thing once and it took over a month for the school to complete. We didn't have a month for the payment deadline loomed. I don't know if evil was prevailing or God working to build my daughter's faith in Him.

I told my daughter not to worry for we will complete the paperwork, then have the faith in God that He would work things out. The day after we submitted the paperwork, which was the next day after we found this status online, my daughter saw where the school had cancelled my loan application. This really got my daughter worried! I tried to comfort her but all my daughter could do was talk about a classmate of hers that went through a verification process that took over a month to complete. I tried to call the school twice but could not get through. I have a photo of my phone that shows on one instance I was on hold for 3 hours but still no answer. I don't think it takes 3 hours to answer a customer service call so I can only assume they weren't answering their phones.

I prayed with my daughter that God would make a way for her. I learned some time ago not to tie God's hands by telling Him how to bless you. Although it was disturbing me that my daughter seemed to have little faith that God would bless her I continued to encourage her that God would bless us to get through this thing in a positive way. My daughter later contacted me and said another friend of her gave her the number to the director of finance and asked if I could give him a call. Before I had a chance to call him, my daughter contacted him herself and reported to me that the school would allow her to continue processing for returning to school while the finance issue got resolved in the background. Wham! Now, didn't God deliver us in a way we never thought?! I later re-submitted my loan package and knew that God would continue to bless us. Everything worked out and my daughter got to see the Glory of God in action!

Another quick story I can tell you is about my son. I've told the story about my son completing college and got a bachelor's degree as an Aerospace Engineer. God eventually blessed him with a job with a government contractor in Virginia. God blessed him with a good job and was being paid quite a bit for a first job after college; however, my son went into this job at a lower pay than what others got elsewhere. I encouraged my son to not worry about that and if he kept the faith, God will either give him promotion on that job or he could later find a job elsewhere at higher pay. My son still loved working at this company but grew a little frustrated for he had responsibilities of what senior engineers would normally do. I encouraged him that this situation would gain him experience that most new people wouldn't normally have a chance to do. My son also worked hard to get a Master's Degree while he worked there.

Not long ago, my son told me about a job opening at a larger government contractor that was located near his job. He applied for the job and felt he had a chance. They later contacted him for an interview. I prayed with him before the interview and he later told me he felt he did really well. Long story short, his experience helped him get the new job with a 28% pay increase! God is so good. So, you may not know why you go through what you go through but God will give it purpose!

The last story here is related to me and my job. I've mentioned how God blessed me with a wonderful job in Tampa, FL; however, I had to leave my family in Georgia for various reasons. I later became concerned that there were people with less experience and education than I getting promoted and I had rarely got beyond the point of applying for promotion. So, in 2017 I applied for promotion and actually made the list of eligible persons for promotion. I was ecstatic! I finally was getting recognition that I deserved to get promoted. I later began to realize that although I would be making more money and would gain more status, getting promoted and moving from Florida could become a problem for me and my family. So, I prayed to God that although He knew I wanted a promotion, to not bless me with a promotion if it would affect my lifestyle and family. When the list came out in January 2018 I was not on it. Believe it or not, I considered this a blessing for God had answered my prayers. One of the guys competing with me ended up getting promoted and going to a country to which I did not want to go. So, you see, not being promoted at that time was actually a blessing. I will continue to trust God in what He wants for me.

This is why when you are going through a problem, never compare your problems to someone else's and never think you're going to end up like them. Through God you will be victorious in your endeavors if you rely on your faith. If you call on the Lord and operate in faith, you too can receive uncommon blessings in a common world!

www.ingramcontent.com/pod-product-compliance
Lightning Source LLC
Chambersburg PA
CBHW060201070426
42447CB00033B/2262